A Book of Advice for the Homies

Wayne Anderson

A Book of Advice for the Homies
Copyright © 2020 by Author Wayne Anderson
Publisher: Creamed Colored Publications

All rights reserved. No part of this book may be reproduced or transmitted in any form or by any means without written permission from the author.

ISBN 978-0-9863178-4-2

Printed in USA

Table of Contents

CHAPTER 1: Mastering the Game of Chess 1
CHAPTER 2: Think like A Boss 11
CHAPTER 3: Act The Way You Want Others To See You 19
CHAPTER 4: When You Depend On Others, It's A Powerful Vice 23
CHAPTER 5: The Power of Negotiation...Getting What *You Want*... 27
CHAPTER 6: Character is everything 33
CHAPTER 7: Friends 37
CHAPTER 8: Thanks for the warning Uncle Wayne 43
CHAPTER 9: The Hustler's illusion 47
CHAPTER 10: What is happening to us? 55
CHAPTER 11: Mass Incarceration "The Greatest magic trick that I have ever seen"... 63
CHAPTER 12: How to inspire little champions 69
CHAPTER 13: The greatest field trip I ever went on... (Experience Inspires) 73
Acknowledgements... 81

CHAPTER ONE

MASTERING THE GAME OF CHESS

When I first learned how to play the game of chess, I sensed that its purpose was far more than just pushing pieces around on a board and enjoying the simplistic outcome of trapping your opponent into a corner, while wasting hours of precious time doing it. I had always been taught that time was money, and if I was sitting around wasting time enjoying a game that had no purpose outside of checkmating someone, then maybe that interest in playing board games defined my character and exposed my true IQ for getting money.

There had to be something more to it. I'd seen too many successful people making moves, whether it was in business or politically that were similar to the strategies of a chess game for their volatile, magical, and masterful outcomes to not be directly connected to the game of chess.

How could it not be? It's the same game we learn in the streets. The same game we run as hustlers while trying to outmaneuver the police on our way to the top, or while we outthink our opponents to own the number one spot on the block. Where it is incumbent for us to be subtle, congenial, cunning, democratic, gracious, and polite; yet scandalous while appearing smooth like a politician. And just as they do in business, you had to move with the paragon of elegance. If you had to cross an opponent, you did it with someone else pushing the chess piece, while you stood back and appeared innocent with a smile of honesty and trust on your face.

This way, you could continually seduce your opponent into a trap with charm, deception, and a conniving strategy, always planning and staying two or three moves ahead of him without him ever suspecting you of wrongdoing, while you silently attack him like a virus in his blood. People do this every day. They act civilized, decent, democratic, and fair, while always remembering that it's just a game being played like chess. This is politics 101.

For example: There's a character that speaks real slow who seems ignorant. Playing Sammy the Bo-Bo is a good game because if he plays his part right, he can rock you to sleep. He's so good at what he does until he'll even try and convince you that he doesn't even play games, because playing games to him is a waste of time, and it's beneath him and sinister, it's reprehensible, and outright wrong. He or she may even pretend to be a religious fanatic.

Of all the players, this is the one that you must be aware of because he'll be the one that gets close enough to you to learn your moves and use them against you to checkmate you. When you believe that he is truly slow, that's all he needs to begin to manipulate you.

Once he detects that you believe he's a slow opponent, his next move is to convince you that you can trust him, that he's honest and straight, and always keeps it (100) "real," because he knows that his game is based upon deceit.

Just think about how relaxed you could become around someone that appears slow and controllable - who appears to be innocent and honest. Without realizing it, this person can work magic on you, and coerce you into a situation or a trap before you know it. Girls do this to guys all of the time. Always investigate the motives of an opponent and since most people are almost always deceptive, would you rather your opponent be the fox in sheep's clothing while you be the victim, or would you rather be a wolf in lamb's clothing?

Never be so naive to believe that a friend or an opponent--no matter how slow or innocent he appears--won't betray you. I guarantee you, if there is not always someone around you in sheep's clothing, then there is one that is a hawk disguised as a vulture, with a buzzard's mentality, circling you just waiting for you to fall, so they can take your place.

The best way to recognize deception is to become a master of deception, not to be deceptive, but using it as a tool and a detector so you won't be deceived. In this way, no one will ever be able to brag about pulling the wool over your eyes. Recognizing deception won't cost you a thing, but not recognizing it can cost you everything.

If you should ever have a problem with the police, a shrewd businessman, or the court system--you will learn at the speed of sound that there is a set of rules you 'must' learn and play by in order to win. No matter what you thought otherwise. So, if the rules of the game are inescapable, then it is better to be a chess master rather than a mediocre player. If you're going to play, then you may as well play to win.

What separates the chess master from the ordinary player is his awareness and his ability to remove his emotions from a situation or the game. One of the rules we follow is that we should always:

"Be swift to hear, slow to speak, and slow to wrath." (To become angry) Never volunteer "extra" information

Always remain calm, and never let an opponent see you sweat!

This is what makes a chess player in the game, a chess master--self-control. Before you can become a chess master you must first learn to master your emotions. An emotion uncontrolled at the wrong time, in the wrong situation can cost you your life. Emotions can cloud your judgment and reasoning, and if you cannot think straight up against another chess master, you will never win.

Anger is the most lethal and costly emotion in your realm of thinking because it always suggests revenge and violence, rather than reasoning. If it's your intention to move in closer to your opponent to trap him, or if you desire to be closer to someone in business who you also see as a potential enemy with the potential to hurt you in the long run, it would benefit you first of all to evade him, but if you must do business with him, it would benefit you far more by presenting yourself as a friend with a smile on your face than it would with a frown displaying anger. Remember: Just as you can draw flies with honey, you can seduce an enemy with a smile.

Mastering the Game of Chess

There is another rule that we follow:

"Love thy neighbor, and hate thine enemies, but I say unto you, love your enemies." (But never trust them)

Love and compassion when given to the wrong person is shot from the same barrel that fires a bullet of destruction, when used effectively by your opponent. They can destroy you, much like the honest face and pleasant smiles of a slower opponent Sammy Bo-Bo. They can blind you and close your eyes to the true intent or the next move that someone is planning to make against you. They can cause a lapse in your sense of security and keen sense of sight, that will cause you not to see that you are being set up to take a fall. It is not supposed to be that way. When you remove your emotions from the game, it clears the path for you to always see what your opponent is thinking. Do a favor for the wrong person, based on your emotions and it can kill you quicker than a bullet.

Once you have removed your emotions, it also makes it a lot easier for you to remove yourself from the spotlight, and out of harm's way. I remember seeing a coin once that had two faces on it. The two faces were the faces of a Roman deity that was able to look in two different directions at the same time. Possessing the skills of this Roman Guardian is invaluable in the game, especially when you're playing chess, because you have to possess the skills to look in front of you, behind yourself, as well as into the future, and then back again into the past while always keeping your eyes opened like the eye that's always watching that's in the center of the pyramid on back of the dollar bill.

If you do this, then nothing or no one should catch you by surprise because you are constantly monitoring your environment like a radar monitoring weather.

This is why it's so important to possess the skill of the Roman Guardian Janus; being able to look into the rearview mirror as you drive forward, not because you fear being followed, but you look back there for the lessons learned over the course of your life. No matter how many books you read, you will never gain more from the lessons of your life, nor will you ever attend a better school that will teach you more because these lessons come directly from your own experiences.

When we look back, we look back at how others before us succeeded, and why we did not, or why we end up broke or in jail and they do not. And once you have extracted the information from the lesson, you make a vow, just like you do when marrying, but with this vow you commit, and conclude that you will never cheat or be cheated.

You do this by writing down the mistake that cost you the most, then you repeat what you wrote down until it becomes a part of your brain. "I will never ever make that mistake again, nor will I ever allow myself to be betrayed through pleasantry and a smile." Whatever the mistake was that costed you the most write it down.

After you have mastered removing your emotions, now comes the magic of disappearing from the game. To do this, you must be willing to see the intelligence and the reasoning for Michael Jackson to have worn his masks out in public. Michael knew the benefits, the effects, and the importance of being incognito. But no one in Michael's life wore a mask more concealing than the mother of his third child, Prince Michael. Until this day, no one knows who she is. That's the one we must master. The one you can't see.

I want you to think about something for me.

How often has God blessed you, or has worked out a miracle for you, and you've whispered, "thank you Jesus!" Instead of reaching over and giving him a hug or bumping knuckles with him, you whisper into the air because you can't see him, but you know He's there because He just touched your situation. So you thank him in a whisper. Even though God is always around and everywhere, no one can ever tell you that they've seen his face. There's a lesson in that. If your enemies can't see you, it makes it hard for them to harm you. They can't harm what they cannot see. It would be easier for them to see air blowing through the breeze than it would be for them to touch someone they can't see. What if Jam Master Jay, Dr. Martin Luther King, Malcolm X, or Stokley Carmichael had known this.

Now here is where we have to remember what we learned from Sammy the Bo-Bo with his game that rocks you and keeps you asleep. As your enemy, he will try and convince you that this is deceit, but beware, because not only is he using a tactic to keep you asleep, but you can rest assured that the lips from which he's speaking to you are from behind a mask just the same. He's the one being deceitful, and you never have to feel guilty about being deceptive because this is really not who you are, it's just a role you must play to keep your opponent off balance, and from stabbing you in the back.

Politicians, cops and some successful people do this every day. You wear your mask not to be deceptive in a bad way, but as a costume that allows you access to your opponent's game plan, which allows you to put a face on the invisible moves that were just waiting in the dark to crush you. Never allow your opponent to cause you to not wear your mask for fear of being accused of deception. Also, you have to remember that this same competitor that calls you deceitful sees this as being sharp when he does it to you, and he also believes that he's outthinking you when you don't do it. If he's mastered the game himself by removing his emotions from the game--then he sees nothing wrong with deceiving you.

While you may feel a little uncomfortable about it at first. That's only because you have never really thought about it this way, and perhaps you've been the victim of somebody deceiving you in a bad way. A chameleon changes his colors to blend in with the environment, not to harm you, but to deceive you, only for his protection from you. Half of the world moves from behind a mask while practicing the art of deception. How do you think Donald Trump won the Presidency? This is why the some will always continue to get rich, because they've learned to deceive the whole world.

When they do this, it starts with their personality (with a simple smile or an expression). Every time that you've seen a woman apply makeup in a mirror, you've witnessed the art of deception, and every time you've seen a woman wear a weave, they are practicing deception. And every time you've gone to the theater to see a movie, you've paid to see deception.

Not because the movie was fictional, but because the actors were fictional. The actors you see on screen are not who they really are, those are characters being paid to deceive you into believing that they are real.

It's like how we--as men--pretend to be so innocent when we first meet a girl, acting unconcerned about our sexual urges, but knowing all along it's our every intention to seduce her. I don't have to tell you how to be deceptive; you already are!

In the crown of the King is a jewel. It's the jewel that every king must have before he can become a master of the game. This is the golden rule; and the ultimate Jewel

"Let patience have its perfect work, that you may be perfect, and complete."

In anything you do, except trading stocks on Wall Street, requires patience. In the game of chess where life depends on the outcome of your next move, patience becomes the wisdom and knowledge you'll need to display your understanding for whatever it is that you're doing. Whether you're preparing to make a substantial investment into a business venture, or you're preparing to regress into hustling; patience is the move you make on the chess board that signifies that you are ready and prepared. Once you develop this skill, when you look back over your life, when it was time for you to make the mistake that would've cost you everything--'patience' will have been the skill that held you down, while making it possible for you to escape.

The life of the king, and almost every other king in the Bible had to learn this lesson one way or the other.

Hear is an example: And they cut off his head, and stripped off his armor, and sent it into the land of the Philistines round about to publish it.

All kings are targets for being beheaded. This goes for all hustlers that are hustling in a cutthroat game. Never forget that it was hate that killed one of the greatest kings of our times-- Martin Luther King Jr. And hate will be what kills you in the game.

And since it is the dream of every chess player to become King, how well you know the rules will determine how long you keep your head from being cut off. So, just as we learn to study and read the numbers on a triple beam, the ability to read those numbers and match work with weight, that same aptitude and skill has to be carried over into the business world to match the rules of trading merchandise for a profit.

In this book I tell the story of how I accumulated my wealth, while making moves, applying my principles and studying the rules. But wait, there is one last rule that we live by:

"Study to show thyself approved."

The way we become self-taught chemists in the kitchen of some old apartment, whipping' and mixing chemical substances like master bakers in a corporate bakery. We have to "graduate" into becoming psychoanalysts. Analyzing and studying like psychologists. We must study those we have competed with, as well as those in which we now compete, while measuring their success against our own. But while we study, we must never forget that no one is above studying, and no one is above distrust. Never put all of your trust into anyone--save some for God!

And though we should suspect our enemies, always remember that it was Michael Vick's cousin who sent him to prison, and T.I.'s bodyguard that set him up. Judas betrayed Jesus, Brutus killed Caesar, Marvin Gaye's father killed him, Roger Troutman's brother killed him, and Christopher Columbus' son killed him. No one is above suspicion. Not our closest friend, not even our next of kin, and never-ever close your eyes, or let your guard down while playing the game. Disregard this advice and someone may just close your eyes permanently.

Tupac, Biggie, and Nipsey--we will never forget you!

CHAPTER TWO

THINK LIKE A BOSS

Sometimes it's not about what you know, it's "who" you know.

As opposed to thinking like an employee, start thinking like an employer. In your home, as a parent you wouldn't act like one of the children, although you might 'think' as they do. You certainly would not act as they do. So I am not suggesting that you start acting like your boss, what I am suggesting is that you start thinking like your boss.

Just as your employer is using his knowledge and skills to manage other people, use your management skills to organize and manage your home front, your finances and lifestyle.

If you are using the techniques and management style of a successful CEO, then you should get the same successful results in your own personal conquests.

This is how you execute what you know, but what if your aspirations are to manage others outside of your home, say for instance, your own business.

You may not have college degrees, but that shouldn't stop you from hiring people that do have degrees. You may not be an accountant or a mathematician, but with the right resources you can hire both.

Just think about the number of scientist, computer programmers, engineers, and mathematicians that were needed to establish Apple inc., but the only name you are used to hearing when it comes to who established the company is, Steve Jobs.

That's because Steve Jobs knew how to use his skills and wisdom to organize the greatest asset a company has, which happens to be people.

Steve was thinking like a boss.

In life, we either own or we labor. You can either sell your labor for money, or you can own a fancy title and work for money. Even doctors and lawyers do this. But the one that owns the buildings, the land and money not only owns the buildings and the land. They own part of your business that's on their land. Therefore, he owns a percentage of your money.

In fact, they own part of your money and your business because they own the way that you produce your income, or sale the things you sell, service, or produce. If you are not an owner, then you work for an owner and owners are bosses.

If Apple and amazon are successful, then what lessons can they teach us?

We should learn to learn from the best.

Learning is what causes us to grow. Every day, in some way we learn something new about technology. And what we learn on a daily basis should not be limited to what we learn about operating Apps and programs on our Smartphone.

Time is precious, and life is short. We still have a long way to go, but only a short time to get there. Therefore, I would encourage you to start your quest to learn as much as you can now.

As humans, we should never allow the hyena, or the buzzard to be smarter than we are.

Just think about this for a moment: you wake up in the morning rushing out of the door and into traffic headed to work, due mostly to a fear that you have about what might happen if you do not earn a paycheck to pay your bills.

As you are rushing to get to work, the buzzard is flying high circling and cruising across the sky with ease, as he watches and waits for other animals, and even humans to do his work for him.

Whether its road kill by a human motorist, or a kill by another animal. After the job is done, the buzzard swoops down and enjoys the full feast of the carcass. He does this as if he'd done all of the work himself.

That's the mentality of a boss. It doesn't matter what you think.

There are only two ways that bosses think: They either take the credit for the company's success; or they share the credit with their employees for the company's success. But more than often they will take all of the credit, which is why you'll always hear 'only' the name of the CEO and not his assistants.

Although this may sound a bit abrupt, or even harsh, but when they're flying around in their G-7's and circling across the skies, or walking thought their 20,000 sq. ft. mansions, they never think about this as long as they can feel that they've paid their employees for the work they've done.

Is this not the same mentality that you see with the colleges that are working collegiate athletes getting rich off them, while not paying them?

It's this mentality that causes us to work on a job for 30 years and after retirement we can't even sustain a life of satisfaction, or afford to live out our dreams.

Now, in no way am I suggesting that you not work or not have a job, but what I am suggesting is that you no longer remain trapped in a slave's mentality as you release yourself into the equal prosperity of a boss.

Here's something else to ponder:

The thinking boss knows that there is always a flying vulture circling and looking for an opportunity to steal his success away from him. This vulture is called a competitor. So no matter who you are, unless you have a monopoly going, you will always have vultures circling you and wanting what you have.

Let us play judge and jury for a moment.

What if I was blind, but I had the gift of imagination to see all things that others could not see, and with this gift I could find things, or at least tell others where to look to find what they were looking for.

Sort of like the way that Google does its searches finding things for you.

Now, what if someone close to me, say for example, my guide, or my handler, knew that I had those capabilities, and every time I exercised my gift that led to a discovery he swooped it away from me and took credit for it.

At the end of the day, who do you believe the beneficiary of the discovery is going to give credit for helping him achieve or discover what he was looking for?

If the blind man never found out that his companion was stealing all of his discoveries, as long as the handler was doing his job as a guide, would he be wrong for stealing the benefits of the intellectual gift of the blind man?

When one learns to steal from the minds of great people, is it the same kind of theft as a thief who has robbed you of your property? Is it ever okay to rob someone of their intelligence?

> *"Everybody steals in commerce and industry. I've stolen a lot myself. But I know how to steal."*
> *-Thomas Edison 1847-1931*

Because we are never taught the difference between when we are reacting due to our emotions, and when our emotions are actually doing our thinking for us, we lose sight of what may or may not be morally wrong or right.

Never be so naive to think that someone close to you who desires a better life is not willing to make this psychological and emotional shift right now to become your boss.

Remember, its one thing to steal the labor of a person, or his idea without paying him, as opposed to stealing the wisdom of another person to get what you want.

When you steal to benefit the good of humanity, it is no longer stealing, it is borrowing. Not one person reading this book would have been upset with the CIA if they had been successful at stealing the Intel of terrorists that flew the two airplanes into the Twin Towers on 9/11.

Is this not what Dr. Martin Luther King Jr. did with Mahatma Ghandi's non-violent philosophy?

One of the biggest hits ever recorded by the late, great Whitney Houston was borrowed from Dolly Parton, I Will Always Love You.

Why do you think books are written? They are predominantly written for you to borrow from the knowledge and experiences of the author. Anyone who has ever taken a lesson from history has already done this, and if you are still learning from someone or something in the past, then you are still doing it. This is a shared philosophy among all successful businessmen. Each of them hire others to do the work for them to further their own causes.

Sometimes the world can be a cold and vicious place, and poverty is at the forefront of those places. This is why I labor and do all that I can to aid and assist in the escape of all who are trapped there to help them discover their own treasure of financial freedom. As many as a few may not find this chapter appealing or like how they are feeling emotionally. The truth is, this is how business goes.

And if you are in any way apart of the business world as an employer or an employee, you have to find and accept your role in the entire scheme of this economic apparatus. These are the brutal facts. We either play the role of the slave or the slave master. Ouch!

Borrowing from others has been around forever.

Why do you think we have so many types of the same products?

Because someone else has elected to copy the wisdom of another's work to make it their own in hopes of making it better. This is what vultures do.

Henry Ford does not build cars himself, but yet his name is the only one that you have ever heard when credit is given for building the Ford family of vehicles.

Borrowing is wrong, only when you steal someone's property, or when you take something from them that causes injury.

This is what every student that has ever sat before a teacher has done. He or she has borrowed from the storehouse of knowledge from the teacher, but no one explains to us how we should use this knowledge once we get it.

Here is another point of knowledge to ponder:

So that you are never accused of being dishonest, deceptive, or untrustworthy, always give credit, and also be kind and show love to the one that you borrowed from.

CHAPTER Three

ACT THE WAY YOU WANT OTHERS TO SEE YOU

How people view you is sometimes worth more than money.

Act like someone with morals and dignity, and most people will treat you as such.

Act like a jackass, and you never have to wonder about how others see you.

The way that you present yourself will oftentimes set the stage and determine how your audience will respond to you.

If you aspire to be treated like royalty, with respect and dignity, then you must present yourself in a manner that will compel your desired response.

It is true, that what you give is what you get back in return. Give respect and in most cases, respect is what you will receive in return.

When you behave as if you are wearing a crown, people automatically sense that you are in some way important.

This chapter was not written to promote arrogance, or to create an attitude of pomposity. I wrote it to uplift you from the ugly grip of poverty. Furthermore, I wrote it to magnify your beauty as a human being.

It was also written to electrify, or shock you into seeing the person that you should be. If you've ever wanted to be treated equally, then the first thing that you should do is act as though you are equal, and above the circumstances you may be in while also maintaining your humility.

There is power in humility. Humility was the force that drove the Civil Rights Movement.

Although black people were punished, beaten and jailed, they always acted with dignity and humility. Through television, the bestiality of their oppressors was revealed depicting them as the animals that they were.

When people see that you are humble, dignified, and trustworthy; trusting you will disarm the most distrusting and ill-hearted person.

There is an esoteric power that comes with being trusted. This trust will take you places. It will place you in circles and open doors for you that would have otherwise never have been opened for you.

Along with his reputation, this was the key that opened the door that allowed Dr. Martin Luther King Jr. into the Oval Office of the White House.

Act The Way You Want Others To See You

When you present yourself as a competent banker, you tempt others to open their wallets to you.

Present yourself as a homeless person, and the most that you can expect is a meal.

Will Smith is one of Hollywood's highest-paid actors. Take your eyes off the movie for a minute and take a look at what I just said to you. Will Smith is one of Hollywood's highest-paid actors because of his ability to act. Acting will get you paid, if you can pull off an act that people can relate to.

I am not saying, "Fake it until you make it", what I am saying is, act like the person that you want others to believe that you are. If you want a life outside of poverty, you must act like it. How you present yourself is how you see yourself.

I wonder how someone can say they believe in God who they've never seen, and not believe in themselves, a person they see every day. When you grow into the person you desire others to see, you're no longer acting because you have become the person that they believe you are.

CHAPTER Four

When You Depend On Others, It's A Powerful Vice

When you depend on someone, it is in that moment that you give them power over you.

Do you depend on your job to pay your bills?

Do you depend on government subsidies for your income?

Do you depend on Social Security or Medicaid for healthcare?

How does it make you feel when you have to wait in traffic?

Why does it not make you feel this way when you have to wait all week for your boss to pay you after you've worked?

How do you think it makes your boss feel to know that you depend on him or her?

I can tell you how it makes them feel. It makes them feel that they have power over you. And this is why sometimes they disrespect you, as if you have no value as a person. When you give people power over you, they will control you in ways that benefits them and their own causes.

If your employer fired you today would he have to shut down his business?

How could your employer be so valuable to you, but you not be just as valuable to him? When you choose to live your life working for others, you choose to give them the power to decide what value will be placed on you.

Some CEO's give other CEO's a different level of respect than they exhibit toward their janitors. Some employers value you based on your skill, your contributions to their success and whether you can be replaced. Whenever you are easily replaced, nothing is lost when you are fired.

Never take your eyes off of the power that you give your employer that he wields over you. When you give him that kind of power without increasing your value, you are always vulnerable to being replaced and as long as he knows that he has that type of power over you, he will always be in a position of control because he can rely on the same fear that causes you to rush out of your home every morning to report to his establishment.

He is the primary provider you depend on to pay your bills, so in that case, why wouldn't he feel this way?

When You Depend On Others, It's A Powerful Vice

In whatever job or position you hold, become so good at it that it increases your worth so exponentially, you cannot be replaced. With your increase in value, comes an increase in respect and less control over you by your boss.

When you increase your value exponentially, roles reverse and now your employer is the one that has become dependent upon you. This is the only insurance that you can have in your arsenal so that you never have to worry about someone firing you. Never let the joke be on you because you gave someone power over you.

CHAPTER Five

THE POWER OF NEGOTIATION...GETTING WHAT *YOU WANT*

The first person that you must convince in the negotiation process is yourself. If you cannot convince yourself, then it is going to be next to impossible to convince others.

In the Garden of Eden, the serpent convinced Eve, then Eve convinced Adam, but before she convinced and persuaded Adam, she had to convince herself.

Eve's personal persuasion came out of her own mind and how she thought. She took from the tree because it was desired to make one wise. She was convinced.

The serpent used the art of persuasion on Eve by offering her something that she found appealing, and in turn she convinced Adam that it was good for food, something that he also found appealing.

Negotiation is an art that completely finds its footing on appeal. Nothing attracts like appeal and interest.

This is the number one deal-breaker between man and woman Appeal.

What can you offer someone that will appeal to their cause?

The serpent offered Eve a chance to become a god, one to know good and evil, and to have her eyes opened.

Eve reasoned, wow! This is a chance to become wise, so why not?

And then Eve took of the fruit, and did eat, and gave also unto her husband Adam.

The serpent executed the art of negotiation perfectly and got what he wanted.

In negotiation, what can you offer?

More money?

More power? Fame and prestige? Safety?

A career?

Love?

Connections?

Labor? Loyalty?

What is it that you can offer someone?

Most times there is always something that you can offer, because almost every person has a need or a desire for something. You just have to find what is needed and appeal to it.

It is the nature of humans to desire.

If you should learn to "mix" the art of offering something that someone else wants, with the request of what you need, you will likely kill two birds with one stone. You give the subject of your offer what he wants, while you receive what you want.

By granting your request, he adds to his own fortune. However, sometimes just offering genuine help without an ulterior motive at the right time is more powerful than any art or science you could ever practice. Some people want nothing from you except a genuine opportunity for them to help you.

When you are trying to overcome poverty, this is the magic that slides you from one end of the poverty line to the other end of wealth.

Take notice of my word selection.

I used the word "slide" as if to imply that poverty and wealth are on the same line; they are, just on opposite sides of the same thing. Both at the extreme of each other consisting of a single thing.

Money.

One group hardly has any, while the other group has plenty.

So, if poverty and being rich is on the same line, how does one slide from one end to the other?

The same way that dusk slides into dawn, or winter into spring. We learn to blend our ignorance about our finances into knowledge about money management.

Ignorance and knowledge exist on the same axis, but on different ends of the mind's axle. Both occupy the same place. The difference between knowledge and ignorance is not location; the difference is in the mind. On one end of the mind's axle it is depleted of knowledge causing ignorance, and on the other end of the same axle in the same place it is filled with knowledge.

However, although ignorance and knowledge appear to be totally unconnected, just as you have the power to slide down the poverty line to the other end of wealth, what if you won the lottery. You can remove ignorance and replace it with knowledge the way that winter blends with cold, or summer with heat.

As long as humans have the ability to change their minds and have the ability to choose and decide, they have the power to change from one end of a thing into the opposite end of what's at the other end.

Love and hate are on the same plane. There is really no difference. What makes love and hate different is a choice to feel one way or another about a thing or a person.

Love and hate both emanate from one source: emotion.

They both are emotions operating from opposite ends of the same emotion that can be changed at the thought of making a decision to decide which one you choose to exert, or display.

Just think of it this way.

Two babies of different races are born, with one being black and the other white.

As toddlers you can place them in the same play pen and they will both display endless love for one another while playing, and will never react to color. But years later, those same babies, now adults, one a republican and the other a democrat, now hate each other.

And that can go both ways. Where there was once no love, can then turn into pure love.

Assume that there is an African American prisoner serving a life sentence for a non-violent drug offense that has filed a clemency with the Obama Administration.

The Power of Negotiation...Getting What You Want

The prisoner files this petition with high expectations that President Obama, being our first African American President, will understand how unjust our drug laws are for crack cocaine offenders. The prisoner's expectations are even higher because President Obama has initiated a clemency project for individuals in this situation, with many of them hoping for relief. This kind gesture by President Obama has won over the love and support of the prisoner as he anticipates that the President will soon grant his request for clemency.

Meanwhile, the prisoner has heard President Trump use obscenities, mock the mentally challenged, and berate women. And as a result, he not only scorns President Trump, he outright hates him.

But as fate would have it, President Obama leaves office and fails to grant the prisoner's petition for a sentence that he knows is unjust leaving the prisoner in custody to die while serving this harsh and unfair sentence.

Two years later, President Trump grants the same clemency request made by the prisoner to President Obama. Just as President Trump granted the request of a 62-year-old grandmother (Alice Johnson), who'd served 21 years of a life sentence. And now after granting the prisoner's request for clemency, the emotional dislike that the prisoner initially had for President Trump, has suddenly changed from hate into love.

This is so because Trump has returned to him the most appealing thing in his entire world.

His freedom.

When you learn to appeal to the most important thing in a person's life, you make it easy for them to say yes to you and to give you what you want. When you tap into what is most appealing to them, you bring down their wall of resistance. No one denies themselves the opportunity to add safely to their fortune when it offers more that contributes to their own cause and desire.

Learn to master this art, and you will find yourself sliding from one end of the poverty line, to the other end, like a baseball player sliding into home plate.

CHAPTER Six

CHARACTER IS EVERYTHING

You can never want out of poverty, find your way out, but then remain the same.

That would be like violating the laws of physics. How can you be in two places at the same time?

If you decide to change your living conditions, then you must also change your image and how you think. Once that is done, it will change who you are.

Most people, if given the chance to extract themselves out of poverty often start that process of change by purchasing a flashy car, and then accompany that with pieces of jewelry. Sadly though, these items and showmanship are not the things that place you on top.

This behavior only shows people how you define your worth and where you place value. We behave that way because we are not taught the difference between placing our net worth in things, rather than investing in commodities that will continuously generate and circulate value within, and throughout themselves. Like assets that keep generating income for generations and inevitably become inheritances for your children, and their children.

* * *

You can learn a lot from Madea.

After Madea has spent her time on stage, Tyler takes her and puts her away as if he's hung up a suit in a closet. Tyler realizes that not only is madea not real, but for a time she had served her purpose. But what stands out most is that Madea is a character and each of us has a character within ourselves. The question becomes, what is the worth of your character?

Madea's is worth a fortune. How much is yours worth?

How we are raised will sometimes diminish our character, thus diminishing our worth along with it. But our worth can be recreated along with our character.

Character is Everything

If our character is worthless, then our personal value will be worthless in a variety of ways.

Although Dr. King has been deceased for more than fifty-five years, we continue to celebrate his legacy because of his character.

Always remember that you have the power to defy, reject, denounce, and repudiate the character that society chooses for you, and society will forever attempt to define who you are if given the opportunity.

Anytime you give the media the opportunity to describe who you are from negative standpoint, they will always describe you in the worst way. You always have the right to choose to deny the limitations that others use to define your character by not giving them something negative to report.

Do you realize that not one successful actor has ever become successful by being themselves? They all become successful after they took on the role of being someone else.

There is a lesson in that. If being who you are has not brought you the success that you seek, then learn to create a character of dignity, intelligence, morality, honesty, and trustworthiness--all noble principles.

Create a character that is totally outside of yourself and this will shine more light on who you really are and could just be the light that you needed in order to move forward.

Here is to shining more light onto something that you already knew.

Life is going to assign you a character role either way it goes. It's called personality.

The problem with this assigned disposition is how much of this role that you are playing has already been written for you. Are you living out a role that is being written by you due to your circumstances, or are you writing your own script as the movie plays itself out?

If you have the God-given power to create your own character, at least create one of worth. Create one that is respected.

Force society to identify you as a human being, and not a statistic or a label or color.

Do not cave into the boundaries that have been set up by a cold and vicious world.

And remember that because you were born into a set of circumstances that molded and shaped you, does not mean that the potter cannot reshape the clay.

You possess the power to reshape and recreate who you are at any given time you desire.

People often mistreat you because you offer character flaws that they find just cause to disrespect.

You can change that.

One of greatest gifts known to mankind is that he has the ability within himself to change himself, and with his ability to change, he also has the ability to change his circumstances and his conditions.

CHAPTER Seven

FRIENDS

The less you socialize with certain people, the greater your chances will be at succeeding in life. Whenever you tolerate idiotic behavior in others, it increases your chances of becoming an idiot. One thing that most all successful people share is their impatience with the ignorance displayed by ignorant people.

As you learn and make changes, your friends should change. I did not say that you should automatically change your friends, but what I am saying is that your friends should also change in terms of their personal growth as you change.

As you change, some of your friends will not want you to change. They will want you to stay put--right where you are--but you must be aware. Friends that do not want to see you succeed will be the first to hate on you when you do. Those closest to us will either contribute to our dreams, or kill them. Just like the weeds in a garden, if these types of friends are not weeded out, they will choke your vision and your will to grow and blossom.

Never allow the seeds of a false friend to take root in the garden of your world and grow, and never reveal your innermost secrets to them for they will eventually eat away at the root of all that you desire, and devour you like a canker worm. Not everyone that smiles in your face has your best interest at heart. Oftentimes, it is the one with the most gracious smile that wants most to see you fail.

With many of the people you spend time with, you spend it teaching them, and others, you learn from. But be careful of the ones that are there neither to learn nor be taught. They have ulterior motives of only bringing you down. These people you must recognize from a mile away as though you saw them through the lens of a kaleidoscope. If you aspire to soar higher heights like an eagle, then learn to recognize the elevator people along the path of your life. These are people that can lift you up to the next level and take you higher.

Wise is the man that has the vision of the eagle, and the heart of the lion, but even wiser is the man who knows how to pick the right people to befriend. If you run with people who have no values, sooner or later you will become a man without values. If you constantly lay down with dogs you are bound sooner or later to also gain the reputation of carrying fleas. You can always tell a man by the books that he reads and by the people he calls his friends.

Many of the people we meet in the streets, who we call friends will betray you quicker than an enemy. We already know what an enemy will do. It's the one we call our friends are the ones that are more likely to harm us.

It is our so-called friends who truly, and secretly despise us. They do this because of their jealously, and envy, and their desire to have what we have, including the power that they see us enjoying when we're on top.

An enemy will stab you in the face and smile about it behind your back, while a friend will smile in your face and stab you in the back.

The word friend is often misused by people like the word love is when used between two people who are drunk. To some, the word friend is only convenient to use when it's beneficial. Remove the benefits and the friendship disappears.

If you ever want to know who your "real" friends are, place them under the microscope and look at them as you would a building, and see how they pan out.

People are like the shingles on a roof. When the wind blows violently against them, they unravel, come apart and fly away in the wind. These are the people that were with you just for the free ride. They never meant you any good, but you tried to help them in spite of.

Holding the shingles in place is the plywood, which stands between them and the trusses. Your truss people are the ones that will stand with you as long as they can benefit from the protection of the plywood. But let the storm directly affect them and they will bend, break, and crumble taking the entire roof down with them.

Standing tall with you through the storm is the wall people. They are always the last ones to go because they are stronger than all of the other so-called friends. They stand with you the longest because some of them really do care and offer loyalty. But once they realize that the shingles are gone, the plywood, the trusses and roof are all gone; they buckle under pressure, and like the trusses they collapse and fold.

These are the people that you have shared your success with. As long as the going is good, they are good, but let the money be gone, and you will see them gone.

The only people that you can ever truly call your friends are the foundation people. These people will never leave you because they are so strong and connected to you, that in times of trouble not only will they hold you down like an anchor, but they will be around to hold you up no matter how hard the wind blows.

After the storm has come and gone, your foundation will 'never' up-root and neither will a true friend. You won't find these kind of friends in the streets. These types of friends are only found in people like our mothers, our children, the right wife, or in someone that has the same kind of love for you that your mother has for you, like an aunt or grandmother.

Friendship and love can blind you. People can change characters as often as an actor on a Broadway changes his costumes.

In the game, there is no wind storm that blows harder than a federal indictment. It is at that moment you get to see who your building people are.

I made the mistake of confusing the shingle people with the real foundational people. I made that mistake because I did not learn about deception while I was learning the game.

I wrote about deception in the introduction because I wanted you to be prepared for it when we discussed it at a later time in the book. You learned about deception at no cost, but for me to learn it cost me everything.

To some people creating confusion is an art.

If they confuse you, they can deceive you. Here's how:

Friends

In that moment of confusion you are blinded and occupied by the confusion and are now susceptible to deception.

When you confuse a friend with a frenemy, there will always be a cost.

If I had paid attention to the rules of the game of hide-and-seek as a child, I would have learned that the game was not only played to find and seek people, but people also used the game to hide other things--like who they really are.

Anytime someone who you've grown to trust gets close to you and is hiding who they really are, it's just a matter of time before you find yourself being a fool. In the game of chess there is no greater move than a fool's mate.

Whether it happens to you in a relationship, in a business deal, or you realize this after you've caught a case and now sit in prison. If you should ever choose to befriend someone who believes in having two faces, or believes in hiding who they really are; I can promise you that they won't disappoint you when the time comes to fool's mate you. This is the friend that you don't find out about until it's too late.

CHAPTER EIGHT

Thanks for the warning Uncle Wayne

There are some people in this world who has power. Whether it came through financial gains, through the cords of judicial authority, or power extended to them because of who they know.

This is a fact.

And there are people with this power who are evil as Hannibal Lecter, and if ever you should offend one, they will use every inch of power and every means available to them to destroy you.

This is a fact

There are some people with this power that's operating from an entirely different plane from the one that you are operating on, and can be as unreasonable as a slave master who has discovered that his wife has eyes for you. You could imagine the fury that would follow that scenario.

Some people hate, and they hate as naturally as you naturally love your newborn baby.

This is a fact.

Offend some of these people and they will spend the rest of their lives and all that they have to make you feel what they imagine you should feel and how you should suffer. And if they should succeed, they explode in joy and ecstasy as if they were a fan of a team that scores the winning touchdown. Your agony is their delight, their pleasure, and joviality. Some of these people hold positions in our society, whereas they can prosecute you for a crime, or arrest you because of a crime.

Some are even business people. Cross one, and you'll know it when you do.

With some of these people, it does not necessarily have to be a crime that ignites their anger and hate towards you. It could be something as simple as an act of ignorance, or you showing signs of extreme intelligence. All they need is a reason for you to become a target, and because of their power, they will do everything within their power to take you down.

This is something you should know, should you ever choose to become a drug dealer, or hustler, or if you go into the wrong profession.

Never confuse one of these people as being weak, or a sucker because they look frail, or appear to be slow. Never judge a book by its cover, and never make the mistake that you can violate one or overlook them as if he or she is a mark or some weak addict that you are used to taking advantage of in the trap or a dark alley.

Thanks for the warning Uncle Wayne

Not knowing who you are crossing sometimes can cost you your life, if not your freedom--all of it!

You must always remember that the law allows those with power to be as violent as a soldier in war, or a terrorist with a loaded AK-47. Violence does not always leave a trail of blood. Violence can leave your mother heartbroken, your kids without a father, and you in a situation without hope.

Our courtrooms are full of violence, just as our penitentiaries are, and just like some of our streets and neighborhoods are.

In your mind, or in a move that you make (as you always have many times before), to you, it may be just routine, but to the one in power it was an act of war. Though it appeared to you to be a small thing, in that instance, do not look for or expect mercy from them, because in that moment the only mercy you'll get is what Osama Bin Laden got from the United States--and rightfully so. And you might say that my analogy was a bit extreme, but ask any prisoner that's serving a mandatory life sentence in the federal system that was accused of selling a small amount of crack cocaine or some other form of drugs am I exaggerating or being a bit extreme.

A man with power and no reasoning is a dangerous man. And society is filled with them, who're just waiting for their opportunity to show you just how powerful they are. However, not all of them enjoy being placed under the spotlight whenever they have to be mean and unreasonable. In that instance, they're the ones that will throw the rock and hide their hand and enjoy the victory of crushing you in secrecy.

Of all the things we learn before entering the game, no one-- let me say that again, no one tells you about these people, or that they are the ones that will be collecting the debt that you must pay for violating the laws of justice, the laws of society, or their interests and investments.

There are some men that wear suits that display Colgate smiles and come across as being the most amicable person with the most jovial personality and behind that smile is a vicious undercurrent of simmering hate that's covering up their desire to be a serial killer. A serial killer who's smart enough not to kill with a weapon, but with the law.

What do you think drives "Mass incarceration"?

So dangerous are the people that both arrest and prosecute you that committing a crime (even if it's for the sake of surviving), it's no longer about bringing you to justice, it's now personal. It's the opportunity for them to release their anger and display their hate to their counterparts and to show the world how powerful they are and what they can do and get away with.

Violate this advice at your own risk, gamble if you like, and if you should ever come face to face with one of, or some of these people--what I've written and what I am saying to you will stand out in your mind as clear as you looking at the words on the pages of this book.

CHAPTER NINE

THE HUSTLER'S ILLUSION

Life is a journey, and as we travel along that journey we should learn. When I was three years old, if someone had given me a pair of shoes to wear that were a size 8, it would've made no sense. But now fast forward that by ten years and I am now 13 and my shoe size is an 8. It would then make all of the sense in the world to now give me the size 8, because I have grown into the moment, and into the right shoe size and that's how life should be.

We should grow moment by moment. Even if we stop growing, we should never stop learning.

It is because of my growth that I now understand what happened to me, and to others like me who all had dreams that turned out bad. Trust me, this goes so much deeper than a group of guys or a certain group of people that made bad decisions to hustle drugs.

As an example of just how deep this goes, let's use Tyler Perry's character Madea. She's the perfect example of how you can create an illusion by using make-up and a camera.

Using both make-up and a camera, they help create the illusion that a man can appear to be a woman, and it's no different from what the streets can do with a dream. They can turn a dream into a nightmare, or better yet, a dream into an illusion that becomes a nightmare.

What nation do you believe is the most powerful in the world?

Is it Russia, China, or the USA?

Neither.

The imagination is the strongest nation in the world; it's through the imagination that those countries were created.

But we have to beware of how we use our imagination, because it can trick us. This is so, because of its power to confuse us. It can confuse us with understanding the difference between a dream and an illusion. The difference between something that is based on what you desire, as opposed to something that appears real, but is not and this misunderstanding is what makes up the illusion the way make-up created Madea.

Dreams are like fantasies that can come true; illusions never come true, they only trick and deceive us.

Growing up in the environment that I came from, it was an illusion that I was chasing and believing it was my dream.

The Hustler's illusion

My dream was to one day be rich and successful. It was the illusion of being able to accomplish that through hustling, rather than the reality of me knowing that street hustlers never become rich without eventually losing it all. Believing that I was pursuing my dream, through ignorance, it deceived me.

Illusions are created to fool, they are not created to make one believe. Besides, if you are fooled, then you believed anyway.

The greatest element of an illusion is the thread of truth that's woven within it that holds it together. It's that sprinkle of truth that shines through like the spark from a diamond that captures the attention, and it's the beauty of the spark that intrigues us and causes one to focus on the spark rather than the illusion. In the game of seduction, this is the move that women always make on men to seduce them.

If beauty is the magic that women use to hypnotize men, then trust must be the lie they tell to conquer him. Wherever there is trust, then there is no need for one to question what he sees. Establish trust, and people will believe what you tell them.

Reality TV shows are extremely popular. Not because of their potential to entertain, but much of what you see is what reflects in your own reality, or a reality that you desire. But so are movies. If you write a movie script that taps into the emotions of people that causes them to identify with the storyline, once they become emotionally attached to certain characters and the content of the movie, a part of them will be persuaded to believe that the movie was real, therefore, they never question if in fact it was an illusion. The movie Black Panther is the perfect example.

The art of creating an illusion is not to fool the mind, but to trick the eyes.

When creating an illusion, tap into the emotions of people and include money and other prizes therein and you will have people flocking to you like bees to honey.

The perfect canvass on which to paint an illusion is on the minds of people who are looking for something to believe in. Religion is the number one painting that people use to draw up their illusions. Religion is number one because it is where we must look for hope and a Savior. We believe in gods that we've never seen; in a statue, a doctrine, or an idea. Some will believe in anything that empowers them. If you're wondering, "I do believe in God."

In whatever it is that will cast the feeling upon them that through believing they will be blessed. Even an illusion and a lie, as long as it promises fortune and fame. Bernie Maddoff and his high-tech Ponzi Scheme is evidence of this truth. More people have been fooled by the illusion of love than by Houdini.

The actors that can bring tears to the stage or the screen are the greatest casters of illusions, even more so than the magician who saws the woman in half on stage right in front of you, and reattaches her without one drop of blood. The actor is even more persuasive than that because every one of us has within their fabric a strand of sincerity, whether it is a child, a woman, boy or man. It's just a matter of striking the chord that's attached to that strand and playing it like a musician plays an instrument. Play the chord, and your audience will never doubt what you tell them, or what you are showing them. They give actors Academy awards for doing this.

Steve Harvey shared a story with his audience about why little boys don't like to take baths. As a child, he said that when it was time for him to take his bath, he would put some dirt in the pockets of his pants, and as soon as his mother was out of sight, he would take the dirt out of his pockets and spread it around in the bathtub, which would create a ring around the tub and it would look like he had taken a bath.

This my friend, is the power of illusion.

The Hustler's illusion

Illusions are lies that are processed through the eyes, which tells the mind what to believe.

Most people lie, so when you do or show them something that appeals to the lies they tell, you need not worry about creating an illusion. Just as he says, she says is real, do this, and people will create an illusion for you through gossip, and repeating everything you said, or by mocking everything you did while passing it along as if it were the absolute truth.

Camouflage creates the perfect illusion to trap animals, but so powerful is camouflage that our military uses it to trap people.

This is the power that we go up against in the streets. In a game that will trick you the way that camouflage tricks its prey by hiding the hunter and concealing the soldier in the same way the con-artist hides the truth when scamming his victims.

A good illusion is when you can lead people into a trap, but a great illusion is when you can lead them into a trap and they 'never' discover that they are trapped, or how they even got there.

The imagination is the movie theater for the best illusions when it comes to misleading and trapping individuals like animals.

The movie Scarface was an illusion with a blend of truth and hope that fooled millions into the game that led them into prison without them ever knowing how they got there.

The music industry has used the rap game in the same way. They've hoodwinked an entire generation to follow an illusion that has transformed their fans into a culture of drug use, violence, prison, and poverty. Where videos and seductive images influence kids to believe it's their way out-it tricks them, and instead of being their way out, it becomes their way in.

This happens because most people that are living in poverty are always looking for a way out, and Scarface and the rap game both "appear" to be the perfect exits. When in fact, they are nothing but traps for the majority of kids who are sucked into the illusion of making it big or becoming rich through selling drugs. They have lured millions through disguised doors appearing to be exits that are nothing but traps, and once they lure their victims through these doors of hope, they close like a door that slams and catches your finger.

It's no different than looking into a mirror, but never realizing that everything you place in front of a mirror is reflected back to you in reverse. No one ever tells you that this is how the game goes.

Consider this illusion: What if one day we discovered that the very same ones that oversee the technology industry are the very same ones over the prison industry, and what if we later found out that those who are over the pharmaceutical companies are also partners in the prison industry.

They could very well be making drugs, and supporting the DEA, while at the same time getting kick-backs from the CEO's of the private prison industry.

Remember, hide the truth by camouflaging it, and no one will ever see what is hidden behind closed doors. Winston Churchill once said, "Truth is so precious that she could be attended to by a bodyguard of lies."

There are people who believe that they can go to Vegas and break the bank, but they never do.

The streets will offer you the same bet, and the same opportunity. So, there will always be people that will hustle always believing they can win the bet. But just as they never break the bank in Vegas, they never achieve their dream of becoming a successful hustler in the streets.

It's a vicious game, a lie, a trick-it's a set-up!

It's your favorite movie with you being the star. Your life in the streets is the movie that lets you see everything that you were

The Hustler's illusion

looking for; it's your imagination in action. It'll let you feel everything you want to feel, see, and touch.

But so does the bait that's swallowed by the fish that will ultimately cost him his life.

The fish that swallowed the bait and couldn't get the hook out of its mouth, is the fish that believed the illusion.

Don't let the money be the bait that caused you to believe in the illusion. Swallow the bait, and just like the fish you lose. This is the power of an illusion.

Go for the bait, and end up just like the fish that prisoner's eat every Friday.

Every Friday in the feds, they feed you the fish that believed the illusion and swallowed the bait. Now how ironic is it that both you and the fish would end up in the feds on the same day?

Does that mean you both went for the illusion and swallowed the bait.

CHAPTER Ten

WHAT IS HAPPENING TO US?

Be lofty if your thoughts and in all that you do. Show that you deserve to be treated like a king, even though you may not be one in reality.

Remember that people will always treat you the way you act.

Which brings me to why we sometimes are treated in ways contrary to how we should be treated. When I was in the streets as a hustler, we respected one another as men. We respected the elders that were on our block, and we respected the kids and kept them off of the block.

Today, the hustlers that came after my era only respect AK's choppin' and federal indictments.

Right along with the CODE, all of the respect is gone. No respect for the community, none for the hood, and none for ourselves.

I'd like to share something with you that I find very disturbing. I would like to show you what some people think they see when they see us hanging out and hustling on street corners.

I recently read a book titled "The American Negro. What he was, what he is, and what he will become", written by Hannibal Thomas. But before I quote him, let me be clear that in no way do I agree with him. As I stated, I am only quoting what he wrote.

"The negro...has a mind that thinks in complex terms; negro intelligence is both superficial and delusive; the negro lives wholly in his passions and is never so happy as when enveloped in the glitter and gloss of shams; the negro represents an illiterate, cowardice folly, and idleness are rife and one whose existence is apparently unable practically to discern right from wrong."

When Thomas wrote that, I wonder through what lens was he looking, and at what people was he speaking about.

Being the proud African American man that I am, initially, it infuriated me that he would have the audacity to think that he knows what it even means to be a black man in America. But then I go back and I look at the new hustlers that I spoke about earlier, and again, I wonder if perhaps he could have been speaking about them. About a group of young men who've decided to be the creators of their own images, their own rules and to live in a way that demonstrates what it means to them to be free.

And as a result, they have become the groups that are constantly being ushered into America's prison system. Young men who have misunderstood their responsibilities to their race. They've disregarded their responsibility to family and community. And because of this misunderstanding, they place more value on a car and tennis shoes than they do their freedom.

Remember, I am only showing what some people think they see when they see you, and how people see you is how they treat you.

Now that we've heard how a white man see's this group, let us look at how one of the most respected black men in our country see's this group.

Randal Robinson describes what he saw when approaching a group while on his way to a speaking engagement.

"I was in Rochester, New York for a speaking engagement when I walked smack into them not two blocks from my hotel its gleaming glass façade mocking them, their circumstance. No other course open to me now, threading my way through them, people I used to know, they me, but no longer. The faces are adolescent but too knowing, old from un-natural experience, at once expressionless and quietly menacing. The eyes, empty of light, evidence the dissociation of battered souls that had given up and left home long ago. Floppy caps turned backwards over rags, pants hanging over haute hood sneakers. It is too painful to look at them now without a language with which to tell them who they were supposed to become before "it" happened. And now they have been caused to forget even that there had been an "it." Now they're menaces to society. He knows this, but not how he became this. He really doesn't give a fuck either. He knows his name, but not who he is. But somebody gone pay! Maybe even this old motherfucker coming up the street looking at me. Wow!

Do we ask ourselves what happened to them and who are they or why do they not care about themselves; their lives; their freedom; or their families? Or do we defend them just because we're from the same hood and we share the same background?

In 2016, during Memorial Day weekend in Chicago, a total of 69 black men were either shot or killed by other black men.

Mr. Robinson is of the opinion that they've lost "it." The human being that once lived on the inside of them. This is what I know to be factual.

Psychologist Abraham Maslov theorized that people have five basic needs: physiological, security, social, esteem, and self-actualization.

Physiological needs are the most basic needs to be satisfied for the essentials of living--water, food, shelter, and clothing. At this moment, with your needs for air and water satisfied, other needs--such as your desire to achieve--are directing your behavior. Let your need for water go unsatisfied and your thirst will pre-occupy your thoughts and dictate your behavior. Without air, your thirst will disappear.

Someone, somewhere figured out how to use those basic needs against us.

The slave went free; stood a brief moment in the sun; then moved back again toward slavery

W.E.B. Du Bois, Black Reconstruction in America.

Someone knew how to orchestrate the perfect set-up; a trap with an invisible hand, in the psychological form of life as we knew it, and one as we should expect. Thereby tricking us into believing that what we were, and what we are experiencing is just

What is happening to us?

another dynamic of life. Poverty can never be seen as if it's just another dynamic for minorities that should be expected.

With this invisible apparatus (conditioned to believe that our response to hunger and crime are due to our own doing, and that we are criminals by nature) as Thomas suggested.

Whenever you strangle the economic necessity and economic flow of one of the most fundamental needs of society--the need for money. Those who are living in those areas where the economy has been choked to death, not only do you suffocate the life line of that community, but you literally are choking the life out of the people of that community. And when you deprive those people of the essentials and basic necessities, they are going to be lured to anything (trap) that resembles a chance to satisfy those basic needs to survive.

It is not rational for anyone to think that a starving man won't be lured into crime even if it's a misdemeanor for the sake of survival. Who wouldn't consider taking a slice of bread out of a grocery store if they were starving?

Am I saying that this response is automatic and 100 percent absolute, of course not; There are many people who are dealt the same hand and choose to fight through not having enough to eat, insufficient clothes to wear and opt to go homeless before committing a crime, but there are others that won't, and when those who won't are responding negatively to a lure and trap that was set for them would be like you catching a fish and then becoming angry at the fish for taking the bait because he had a need to survive and you just happen to use his need to survive against him.

As W.E.B. Du Bois stated, in reality, was the slave turned back toward slavery because he was ill-equipped to survive in a world outside of his habitat of plantation dependence, where society still discriminated against them, just as the (socially engineered criminal) who is released from prison and not given the necessary tools to cope with and survive in a world outside of prison that is continuously discriminating against him while thwarting his every effort to be included and to survive. His label as convicted felon is his badge of disgrace that identifies him as being untrustworthy and unfit for society even after he has paid his debt to society.

Just as the slave stands in and basks in the heat of the sun momentarily enjoying his freedom. After the prisoner is released, he soon turns back toward his old ways, not because he wants to return to prison, but to satisfy his needs to survive.

At this point, I would assume your question to me would be, am I defending and making excuses for them.

Defending them, yes; making excuses for them, no!

What I am saying is whenever you have people who are being denied a quality of life that provides their basic needs, those people are going to be agitated and angry, prone to violence and open to commit crimes, whether those crimes are against those who are closest to them (black on black), or against the property of others. In these manipulated social conditions, drug dealing is a given and a sure lure for people situated in this situation, especially when it will put food on the table. According to Marlov, humans devote all their efforts to satisfying their physiological needs until they are met, and when someone knows science and psychology to this degree, they can manipulate and/or dictate your behavior in a way that will almost predict your response.

For the most part, your response was not only manipulated, but is here by design.

If by chance you purchased this book and feel that you've paid a price, I pray that you also feel that it was by far worth it. You have no idea how much I appreciate your support. But while you relish on the expense that you incurred from the purchase, please consider that learning what I have shared with you cost me "everything."

I only wish that I could have picked up a book like this twenty-five years ago, and read what you have been privileged to read today. If I had, my entire life would have been different because of my own quest for ceaseless unending wisdom, truth and knowledge, and above all else, intelligence. If you did get something from reading my book and feel that you could use just another chapter or two, I have included two bonus chapters. By no stretch of the imagination could we leave out the children. So we gave them a chapter all their own.

Hope you enjoy!

CHAPTER Eleven

Mass Incarceration "The Greatest magic trick that I have ever seen"

Recently I was watching the Steve Harvey show and his guest was a magician whose name was Kid Ace.

Kid Ace talked about the first magic trick he ever saw. He said that after class one day, one of his teacher's showed him a magic trick. He said the teacher stuck a handkerchief inside of his hand and made it disappear. And that was how he got started.

He then asked Steve had he ever seen a magician standing at center stage where smoke surrounded him, and then he disappears only to show up in a different location in the building.

Kid Ace decided to show Steve how it is done.

First, he drew an 'X' on his own hand as if it was the magician. Then he asked Steve to make two fists. Next, he asked Steve to choose between his two fists. Steve's choice was his left hand. Kid Ace then asked him to place his right hand behind him so it would be out of the way. Kid Ace then placed the hand that he'd drawn the 'X' on top of Steve's left hand, removed it and asked Steve to open his hand. When Steve opened his left hand, the same 'X' that Kid Ace had drawn on his own hand was now on the inside of Steve's hand, and was no longer in the hand of Kid Ace. The whole audience went wild. It was an amazing magic trick.

But I know of one that's far more tantalizing and mesmerizing than that. Let's see if you can figure out this trick.

Michelle Alexander, whose bestseller "The New Jim Crow", helps us set this trick up by stating, drug offenses alone account for two thirds of the rise in the federal inmate population between 1985 and 2000.

Approximately a half-million people are in prison or jail for a drug offense today, compared to an estimated 41,100 in 1980--an increase of 1,100 percent. As a result, more than 31 million people have been arrested for drugs of some sort since the drug war began.

In two short decades, between 1980 and 2000, the number of people incarcerated in our nation's prisons and jails have soared from roughly 300,000 to more than 2 million. By the end of 2007,

Mass Incarceration "The Greatest magic trick that I have ever seen"

more than 7 million Americans were behind bars, on probation or on parole.

When we see the magician place the woman inside of the box and then he saws her in half and reattaches her, we should ask ourselves, now how in he hell did he just do that?

It's magic I'm telling you.

Imagine this. In 2018, President Trump signed a clemency petition led by Kim Kardashian for Grandmother Alice Johnson who served 21 years of a life sentence. Ms. Johnson has a new book entitled, "After Life".

In her book, she expounds on her trial proceedings. She explained that during her trial, her attorney, while cross-examining a witness and asking him to identify Ms. Johnson, couldn't. He pointed at an entirely different person. And since he'd been testifying that he knew her, he should've at least been able to identify her. She also stated that after he pointed out the wrong person, the whole courtroom erupted into laughter because everyone, including the jury, knew that he was lying. And then he did it again, while another witness was asked to point out her house on a map and couldn't do so after he pointed at everywhere but her residence. In the end though, that same jury found her guilty and convicted her of conspiracy to distribute a 1,000 kilograms of cocaine and the judge sentenced her to life.

In 1993, I was charged with conspiracy to manufacture, possess and distribute cocaine. The indictment did not allege an amount. In fact, there was no amount. Whenever there is no amount--it's referred to as "ghost dope". Ghost dope is exactly what it implies. The dope is not there, it's only imagined, so it's called ghost dope.

Shortly after I was charged by federal indictment, I was sentenced not to one life sentence, not even two or three, but FIVE life sentences. When that happened, I don't even have to tell you what I asked: "Now how in the hell did they just do that?"

Well, it has taken me awhile to figure it out. Twenty-six years of equating and calculating to be exact. I have figured out what many are still being fooled by. The greatest trick I have ever seen.

Its mass game, being played in a magical way on the masses of people.

But before I give you the potion to this magic trick, I'd like to share something that I find to be so amazing. I often ask myself the following question: how can a system of slavery exist in the 21st century, that's arresting, shipping, and warehousing millions of human beings in clear view, and no one it seems, out in society sees it. Well, they certainly do not act as if they see it.

Amazing!

Magical indeed!

I guess we have the media in part to thank for that. That just goes to show you how hypnotizing and powerful the media is. The media has a way of over-dramatizing crime whenever the crime is attached to a black or Hispanic suspect. As they are reporting crimes all day--every day.

They'll have you believing that every person accused of a crime is guilty. The media, with its ability to present you in such a sordid and horrific way, convicts you before you ever have a trial. They have you believing that everyone that has been arrested, deserved it. Because they've methodically manipulated us into associating every arrestee or person accused of committing a crime with the image we've seen in the news.

So amazing is this mass movement to re-enslave individuals, that scores of buses filled with prisoners/drive right past

Mass Incarceration "The Greatest magic trick that I have ever seen"

civilians, often through neighborhoods on their way to these disguised plantations, or we drive past these make-shift prisons every day, and the thought of mass incarceration, or modern day slavery in the 21st century never crosses our minds. Whatever they are using to cover that up or to stop one's mind from even thinking such a thought...is powerful!

This is what I know about power. There has been times in history, such as now where a regime has so much power, when they use it, it can cause almost whatever is in front of it to submit (such as Hitler's regime, or Stalin's regime), as it does so magically. People and things will fold in the face of this power like fire that was doused with water.

In my most humble opinion, I have no doubt that slaves can be manufactured, and engineered. For example: say for instance you and your significant other gives birth to a baby boy. Chances are, If he's born in an urban community, his zip code alone makes sure that he is poor and because of an inferior education system that is not equipped to hold his attention, he comes away ignorant of some of the most essential things that will be needed to survive. Because of his status and lack of education. Knowing that he is ill-equipped to survive, they use his will to survive against him. Because of peer pressure and what he's seeing all of his TV role models have, added to his own appetite to survive, he will be attracted to the game to hustle and when he does that he'll be lured into a trap that is waiting for him. The trap is the law that criminalizes anything that he does in the streets. They even make sure there's just enough money to keep him coming back, but never enough to get rich, and if you happen to find a way to get rich, they have forfeiture laws that allows them to take what you have. **Consider this:**

The Thirteenth Amendment

Neither slavery nor involuntary servitude as except as a punishment for crime whereof the party shall have been duly convicted, shall exist within the United States, or any place subject to their jurisdiction.

Did you hear that? Slavery can exist legally in 2020, if they can convict you of a crime.

CHAPTER TWELVE

How to inspire little champions

Tyler Perry has a new book out entitled, "Higher Is Waiting."
   Recently, I was reading through it and he made mention of his son. Because I know how tender Tyler's heart is toward his son, well, toward people in general, I am careful to use the demonstration regarding his son only to make a point that I believe will inspire anyone that reads my book, or his, and after they've considered what I am about to say, I know this is all that Tyler wants to do, whether it is done through his work or my own.

In Tyler's book, he speaks about the life that he wants for his son, he writes: "In direct opposition to how my father raised me, with my own son I focus on being a parent who is tender and loving, attentive, curious, supportive, patient, and aware. I'm not perfect," he writes, "but I strive to keep my heart open and loving. I've sworn never to utter an unkind word to my son, Aman."

He continues: "One day I was walking through the house with Aman, and I was in a hurry to pick something up in the next room. But on our way, my son got totally captivated by what was right in front of him. With typical toddler focus and fascination, he stopped in his tracks, pointed, and cried out with utter joy, "papa, look! Piano! Piano!"

I was in a hurry, but I made a conscious decision not to rush him and to respond to his enthusiasm. I followed his cue, pulled out a bench, helped him climb up, and gently placed his fingers on the keys."

Tyler's love for his son continues. "My intention is to support my son's dreams, encourage him to explore whatever captivates him, and join him in his wonder."

"Which reminds me...Aman and I were walking through the garden one day, and he said, 'I want to bring mommy a rose, without hesitation, I clipped the rose, made sure there were no sharp thorns, and handed it to him."

Before we continue reading, can I at least get you to agree with me that the life Aman is living is one that we all must envy? Nowhere in my entire life have I ever had the initial opportunity to have the life that Aman is having and experiencing.

Through my own brief experience into a world that I got to peek into briefly when I accompanied my mom whenever she would take me to work with her in the suburbs of her employer's home where she was a maid for them. I got to see that there existed an entirely different world from the one where I was being raised. And now, Tyler has presented even more evidence of this other world and the need for us to be exposed to it.

CHAPTER Thirteen

THE GREATEST FIELD TRIP I EVER WENT ON... (EXPERIENCE INSPIRES)

You have to take kids on field trips, but not just any ole field trip. Kids that live-in low-income areas, especially those that are exposed to poverty.

As you read this chapter, I want you to remember the comparison that I made between my life and how I grew up in comparison to how Tyler Perry's son Aman is growing up, and you'll see clearly what I mean, and why I wrote this chapter.

You have to take them on trips into another world to expose them to a "better world." We have to allow school to be an experience (like your first crush) and not just be a place to go as a starting point for learning their ABC's, or to hang out with their friends.

The experience has to teach them unequivocally 'why' they need an education, why they 'need' science, math, social studies, computer science, and language arts.

And sometimes showing them in a setting outside of the classroom is much more effective than just explaining it out of a book. In reality, showing them is to teach them. Life itself is a place for learning, not just the classrooms. The world is a classroom.

Ultimately, solely teaching them these subjects are not enough, we have to teach them how to utilize these disciplines in a real life setting to advance their understanding as to the value and need of these subjects and why they are so essential to humanity.

Once they've gone on one of these life-altering excursions and have been exposed to this other world that they've only seen through the monitor of a TV screen that ultimately inspires them. Whoever is tutoring them must show them convincingly that it was school that made owning the big house they just visited possible, or the business they visited, the cars they saw, and the mega-portfolio they just perused through only happened because the owner stayed in school.

The way Tyler is raising Aman is a blueprint for success not just for Aman, but for 'any' child that is exposed to that way of life. I am an avid believer that you can program the mind for success just as you can prepare it for failure by not programming it to succeed.

If ever an athlete, or successful business mogul or any professional should play host to one of these field trips they

The greatest field trip I ever went on… (Experience Inspires)

mustn't make the mistake of allowing a student to believe that he or she has achieved the success that they have based solely on talent, because it is at that very moment a child becomes mesmerized by all of the material things he sees and the image that the athlete or the professional is displaying as opposed to the role that school has played in his success.

As teachers who are being looked upon by kids as role-models, we have to almost trick them, if need be, into becoming mesmerized with their school subjects rather than by these iconic images, and personalities.

We have to find a way to explain to our fans and admirers that it was school that made everything they see in terms of our success possible, we have to show them wholeheartedly that had we not stayed in school, that none of anything they saw, could have ever happened.

Sometimes even professionals get caught up in the hoopla of their own personas and the fanfare of their success that they miss the opportunity to inspire or have the intended effects that the student should have gotten from the experience of being in their presence, and we end up doing more harm than helping.

Now the student drops out of school, takes to the streets often joining a gang where he tries to emulate the lifestyle of the athlete, rapper or even the professional through illegal means, which will always lead him into the system of injustice. Take it from me, I know.

Our message of success to inspire must never get lost in our own self-centered views and arrogance, or in the clouds of our success; the message must always be clear. If we had not stayed in school, we could not have graduated and gone on to the next level. Staying in school made winning a scholarship possible and being in school made being in the right place possible to be drafted, or at least it gave me a chance to have a better life.

This is also relevant for the girls (although they should learn to stand on their own independence). The wives of these great superstars also had to be in school to meet these talented guys who have elected to serenade them with great lives as the mother of their children.

For example: if Michelle Obama had not stayed in school, she may have never been in the position to intellectually attract President Obama or become the first black woman to ever live in the White House as the First Lady.

Growing up, because of my mother I was fortunate enough to have been exposed to the experience of going on one of these field trips that 'should' have changed my life, but I had no one to explain to me what to do with the experience once I had been inspired.

So I did the wrong thing with that inspiration. Although my mother had done her job to make sure I was exposed, my mom was a maid with hardly any education, and although she had my best interests at heart, that still did not qualify her as the kind of teacher that I needed to reach me and penetrate the depth of ignorance that I was operating under.

I did not have a second teacher to specifically make sure I understood the experience or inspiration. However, I did respond to both the experience and inspiration just as my mother hoped I would, but what good did that do when I was not given a clear understanding of that experience or alternatives that would help me duplicate the experience of being successful.

There was a part two to my mother's plan that she had not considered, and that's the part that I am writing about today.

The greatest field trip I ever went on... (Experience Inspires)

At my age, because I had grown up seeing just as many people selling drugs as I did that were working, I could not distinguish the difference. Poverty not only influences one's decision, but it also blinds. I had no idea that drugs were as horrendous as they were, until much later in my life.

The main problem that a child may have after going on one of these field trips that inspires him or her, is that, without a teacher that knows what the child is seeing through the eyes of a child, and what that child is feeling based on his own personal experience of living in poverty or inside of a world that is filled with pain that offers no way out.

Once they return home from this trip, they may have no one to follow in the community other than a hustler that he mimics to achieve the success that he now desires. Either way, our children are going to be inspired by something. But if he is fortunate enough to be inspired from having gone on one of these field trips, let's say, like into the home of Bill Gates, or he gets to visit my future dream of one day building a Fantasy Land for children where they can go and have the experience of becoming anything they wish to become just for the experience.

It is my dream to build a studio in Florida as Tyler has in Atlanta but do it in honor of the children. This idea was inspired by the senseless shooting death of a six-year-old by the name of King Carter that was fatally shot in Miami, during the month of February 2016.

Fantasy Land would be a place where children from all over the world could come and be assured of the same safety that is offered to the President of the United States by the Secret Service.

It is my personal ideology, that since we are in the business of making movies, producing stage plays that allows us the capabilities and resources to constantly create scenes that bring into reality the visions of the imagination that creates an entire world on film and stage. We can undoubtedly create a fantasy for a child.

Our purpose is to inspire the child and change their lives, one fantasy at a time. My desire is to do with every child that visits Fantasy Land what Tyler is doing with his son, Aman, at home.

This is what a great field trip should do. It should inspire.

Although our business is centered around making movies and producing plays that entertain while educating people, our core value and purpose will "always" be to provide a safe haven for children.

Your character was created by your thoughts. Your thoughts are the spiritual you in the exact character of who you are physically.

The world around you is one gigantic thought. The universe is an even larger thought. Through thought we expand both the world and the universe, even if it is called a discovery, we must discover through thought, understanding, and intelligence.

Think Godly, and God will guide you in your thinking. Intelligent thinking will cause you to become an intelligent person. Think obscene and silly thoughts and you'll become a silly and obnoxious person. Dream of angelic dreams, with visions of a superhuman outcome, and you will get superhuman and extraordinary results.

Your mind is the soil that is the foundation for the seeds planted through thoughts by which you will grow into the person you will become. Fertilize the seeds of your mind with healthy thoughts, and your life will reflect the beauty and culture of a well-kept and cultivated garden. Refuse to fertilize it with healthy thoughts, and it will produce for you a life that's reflective of a garden that's uncultivated and infested with weeds inundated with problems, confusion, and disappointment.

The greatest field trip I ever went on… (Experience Inspires)

Poor thoughts produce poor results. Poor results produces poverty.

Think heavenly thoughts and a source from heaven will guide your steps.

Think from the top down and you will automatically be on top. Think from the bottom up and you will find yourself forever climbing a ladder that seems to have no top.

If you follow these principles, nothing will ever take you by surprise. Imagination is the mentor that counsels your thinking. Think it, imagine it and become it. If you can think it, and imagine it, you can be it.

Follow your dreams, and you will become the vision that you see. Think thoughts that will make it happen, and what you saw in your dream, you will become.

Remember: Any dream that's backed by the right plan can come true.

A dream without a plan is only an illusion.

Acknowledgements

Normally it is in the beginning of a book where you acknowledge the individuals that made special contributions to your work that are worthy of recognition. But I have chosen to go against tradition and acknowledge my contributors here.

To all of you that intentionally caused me pain, heartache and despair, for those who contributed to this torture and experience with your efforts to ensure my demise; where it seems that I should despise you-"I don't".

In fact, I appreciate you and all of your attempts to destroy me. It was actually a job well done by all of you. If it were not for you, I would have never written this book , earned degrees, learned other languages, to be recognized by officials in the White House; which has also allowed me the opportunity to wake others up to who you are. It has also afforded me the opportunity to help thousands of others realize what is going on in our criminal justice system, on our streets, and in the back rooms where deals are being cut to facilitate in your destruction and castration.

Because of your attempt on my life, it has given me an avenue to show others how they may get back on track after finding themselves in a trap that was set by those that are closest to them. Don't be hoodwinked....what appeared to be our decision and our decisions alone that lead to our failure isn't so. We had help....invisibility and hidden powers are real. Game is real, and so is jealousy, envy and hate. There are individuals with super intelligence that are always willing to play the background where they can pull the strings that will forever lead to your destruction.

If it were not for the jealous, the envious and those that wanted to see me fail. I wouldn't be as conscious as I am today.

To all of you who made contributions to my awakening.....Kudos!

Thank you. None of this could have ever been possible without you.

To those of you who unknowingly help me wake up a nation....I applaud you!

Your help has assisted me in completely turning my life around.

And finally, I just want you to know, what you intended for harm has turned out to be one of the greatest blessings I could have ever received.

You woke me up!

www.ingramcontent.com/pod-product-compliance
Lightning Source LLC
Chambersburg PA
CBHW020702300426
44112CB00007B/475